A COLLECTION OF POEMS

WAR PAINT

PATRICK D. HART

Preface

I needed a bed to tuck the monsters underneath. I found myself expelling every crippling thing onto paper, like I was feeding my soul with ink. That's why I started writing. I guess I could have learned how to fold paper cranes, or attended another seminar on how to stop using thumbtacks to control my anger, but I digress. Do you know what it's like to feel so unclean that you try all the wrong things to get a smidge closer to "purity"? If you do, then you can connect to the poems and prose that you're about to read. This book is my distillery. Was my distillery? It is, and was, and always will be. It's my everything and nothing.

Oh, along my journey I also wrote some positive pieces and placed them in here, for there is always a silver lining.

Acknowledgements

To my wife for being that silver lining. To be frank, this book wouldn't have materialized if you hadn't pushed me to recognize its potential.

To my family & friends for being delicate when I needed it, and for being firm when I was being too delicate.

TABLE OF CONTENTS

TABLE OF CONTENTS

TABLE OF CONTENTS

THE THINGS THAT KEEP US

CHAPTER ONE

On Writing, On Living

I don't live here. I live in a child's tears and a mother's pain. I live in the notes of a psychiatrist. Filed away. I don't live in this place. No. I exist in Salem Witch Trials and the Second Law of Thermodynamics. I'm color blind, but find understanding in the red light district. A Polaroid playboy where the camera lens is a best friend; it captures the truth when no one else is looking for it. See, I don't live where you live. I live in you, he and she, distinctly. The tread on my shoes is worn from centuries of time beneath them. Though I am twenty-eight. For the unheard, the misinterpreted, and the challenged criminal of rebellion thought; it's for you that I create.

Time (Miracle And Mistress)

Dusty old pans
I see you through
Old bottles of honey, half used—
Into lonely winter
We travel on winds exhaled,
From cherished memories
Nurtured bravely between our extremities

Slow down your speech
Let down your hair
We can't un-sip summer

Time is both a miracle and a mistress
We all flirt with,
She comes to haunt us
Virulent and cuckolded—
Peeling lines off our palms;
They belong
To the verse we've been allotted
In the womb of her song

Wild Dogs

The wild dogs run
And I watch them run
There are hooks in my back
I feel the spool positioning
—reeling me
Back in, to face the things that created me
What's funny
Is the vacancy of it all
And how the conversations smell
Like dried glue
I watch burning ends of dead discussions
While naming saints alphabetically
To get you through
    While forgiving myself actually
That's the difficulty of speaking from empty pews
Begging is dirty literature spit from integral lips
Hoping is lusty sin read from conviction script
    Give me the obsessive
    Give me the fortified anti-iconic
    Give me the loyalty submissive
    Give me the gravediggers
Begging to be buried with their shovels
I'll drink coffee and ask God to watch the children
This time, at least—
He can try again.

A Dozen Pink Roses

You were blush
Piano wire and energy
Put up with my chewed fingernail beds
And bathtub talks
The only place I acknowledged safety

You were love
Chalk before rain
And the fingertips that wrote grace
On my cheek
The night he passed away

> I miss you like a pulse
> I miss you like sight
> I miss you like youth

You are serenity
Punishment and light
Paint peeling, begging for wash
But I can't bring myself to patch
The wall where our frame hung

The dog still waits by the door
I cry when I see him limp away
Because I don't' think you knew
What you meant to him

I guess now, in a way
We're both strays

A dozen pink roses every Sunday
For you, my love
A dozen pink roses every Sunday

The Thirteenth Rose
(Making Love To A Ghost)

The Memory Contoured
And I sat, confused
A hand and its veins
Once held the shape of time
Outlining pace and place
It gave divinity definition:

I knelt in the face
       Of that religion

There was a plague in the paradigm.
Pink roses signify
The curse of expanding intervals
And all the broken clocks
My mind recesses between
For—
Every fourth East Coast ocean season
Forces my limbs to wrap around you
Like a house on fire
Again
  And again
    And again

Something about that Atlantic salt
      I prefer in pharmaceutical amounts
To season my skin
      With bits of you again

Too much of life is making love to a ghost

Dead Gardens

A modern guttermouth born with a body count
My first aid kit was short a bandage
When my heart started hemorrhaging
It was an arterial sport
To rearrange the times I tried to kill myself
Wait. That's something I'm not supposed to write about
I spent decades drinking hemlock soaked in water
Trying to dilute it
    To transcribe my darkness as something different
Now I understand
That we're all versions and copies of
Moments still virgin in the moment
See—Dead gardens do exist
I keep mine in the pit of my stomach
Like perennial weeds
The remnants of things I loved
Keep regenerating
    I have lived many life-cycles
    Adoring and letting go
Of dog toys; of maple syrup
Of siblings; of friends
Of sunshine; of love itself

Grief

Belief
In a simpler time
Sycamore bark
And picnic grapes
Plucked from the vine
Before
Leather became skin
And grief
Was a tangible thief
Although
I can name it;
I will never own it

Absent Things

The Things No Longer There
Are What We Tend
To Feel The Most

We Shared The Same Eyes

We stare at rocks from playground buttons
You and I—
We had the same eyes

I scrape my knee at the same concerts
To show you I haven't let go
And never will
Your guitar hasn't been strung right
Since it moved into the spare bedroom
I don't find your ghost in there
Because it lives inside of my headphones

I find your face in outdated calendars
And in stained glass reflections
You once said
"Divinity only survives in a Catholic Church
On an Irish hillside"
--one day I'll go there
When I have the strength
And time

Someday I'll understand how children
Forgive God
For removing the marrow from their bones
                    He took half of mine
                    And I swear that it shows

We had the same eyes
You and I

Ache

Virtue has a price
Usually in the sound of a childhood name
That hangs like an echo from the lips of the deceased

I hate mirrors
Because "ache" became a tattoo
Existing in a thick veil of its own vanity
And that weeping mistress
Likes to get drunk on cheap wine
And pretend she knows the definition of sanity
While finger-tipping our own misfortunate legs
In the wake of mortality

A Fracture, A Dancer, A Scrub Jay

I am a fracture
A one legged dancer
Xanax cut with ephedrine
My pores are clogged
With wax from your royal tongue
Corn starch and food coloring
Halloween on amphetamine's

I am a scrub jay
Your organ collected
Playing keys to the tune of its beating
A fingerprint from a ghost
Wiped clean from my liquor dream
Luminal exposing
My thick thigh soup can carvings
Aged on behalf of my brother
And my best friends ghost
Walking hand in hand with their drunk driver

People Still Miss You Saint Michael

There's a black dog nipping at our heels
Like death labeled Achilles after something
Handcuffed and hell bound

The bloodline was wheel chaired at midnight
When you buried Kings in your temple
(Did you pray first?)
The northern lights went dim
And destiny became a fairytale—Grim
      But there I saw a light
      Some say it was a gift
      I say it was a divide

The only valuable thing I ever owned
      Was time with you
      And a wax sealed envelope

When I cried at your headstone
An ocean was born with automatic weapons
Firing from middle earth
I swore it your middle name
And—
Butterflies carried you to heaven
To drink with Gods and Generals

Angels bring you Jameson
Bartenders do me the same
On good days, they even share your name

Apprehension

Start and stop. Stop and start.
Eggs over medium
Microwave mecca in my bedroom
I can't finish a thought
The way I can't leave this house
Why do I always water my garden in doubt?
Something about the way anxiety blooms
It's a violent rush of uncomfortable self-love
Knee bent in the corner
Scribbling my name
Like I must remind myself why I wake each day
Black chipping finger nail polish
And Something Corporate
Nostalgic notes on roller skates
Down the road
To a place I've purposefully ignored for 1012 days
Until now—
Until the shower rained blood
And I was suddenly harboring a sandpaper tongue
Until now—
When my lost limb
Showed up in a dream
And I chased it
To lucidity

Duality

I have this friend
A doppelganger really
He plans spa days in sauna suits
On desert mornings
Dangling us from sayings like "God willing"
And I would give anything, really
To pretend like he doesn't know me
But we—
Exchange headlights for headstones
On Nashville nights
And eat glass like we know our bodies are
replaceable
Substituting romance for remorse
Because the brothers we knew
Took the best of us to the pharmaceutical
At the bottom of the swimming pool
And this friend—
Has more power than I'd like to admit
He remembers his mother's cantaloupe eyes
When I found her
Surrendering to a wishing well
In the attic,
Swinging by her neck by something that didn't fray
Fast enough to save her
If that isn't a parallel for us all
—Than I don't understand peril

The Orphanage

Ran out past the chain link fences
High fiving Russian linguists
Who wore lip gloss and heels
Beneath a bloated moon
As speedy Nigerians
Plucked chickens and readied the vans

Age six and the salt ponds carried me already
With the breath of the un-brushed orphanage
Where moldy walls painted in dreams—
They all looked the same to me

I crawled the vent shaft fogged with love breath
I lust like a steal
Only from churches

       Because they make up in serenity
       What they lack in security

A spoon full of paradise
Heated under my sophomore slump
Like ten years wasn't good enough
Lost in drama, drugs and friends
Who knew me well enough to make
It all taste like heaven or lemon
    Depending on your definition

The road to happiness has always been intersecting
That goddamn orphanage

Tourists In Love

There are always tourists,
Even in Love

Art Store

I wander into the same art store every Saturday after morning coffee and browse. I never buy anything, which upset the owner for the first few months, but now I think we have a mutual understanding. I touch each piece as if my own hands painted it.

Some beautiful things only maintain their beauty in the place they were first found beautiful.

Music can be carried. Books can be carried. People, and a few other things are perfect only in the moment that made them so. My last relationship was this way. Love in abundance, but the shine dulled when we tried to force it into a new environment; when we tempted its movement at a new tempo. I've never wanted to murder something beautiful, but I understand what that is like now.

So, I wander into the same art gallery every Saturday after morning coffee and browse. I don't buy anything, leaving the beauty exactly where I found it.

Keeping it alive.

I Used To Fuck Harder

I used to fuck harder

Now my reflection is in a raincoat
Dragging smokes and flaccid shadows
Down childish afflictions
While begging my bones to do something
—DO ANYTHING
More than fall knee over knuckle,
But that's me on whisky
A natural disaster spraining ankles
With dried ink—
Tying cherry stems of unborn mistakes

My potential limped away with men
Who will take advantage of you
I display confidence
⠀⠀⠀⠀But I am a chipped statue
My crazy gut checks me
As I stuff good pride in unsealed envelopes
It shows up like semen on dark colored clothes

....I used to fuck harder

The Limp

Matchsticks and handcuffs
We're all almost dead insects
Sucking life from an empty can of Raid
I looked inside the purpose of plague
And saw meaning
Something about death brought me to life
I heard that in a song once
The frequency of a serpent seeking God
Gave me a blister on my foot

It still hurts when I walk
I named that limp after you

Appropriate Deaths

I envy appropriate deaths
Not those of seasons
Or relationships

To some
Rotting cheese and discoloring honey
Still tastes sweet
      Like digesting a memory

To me
That vestige
Is stale love stomped, continuously,
Into New Orleans streets

I beg to recapture naivety
      And long for longing
Because it would mean
I have something to lose

I'm just too used
      to the loneliness of abuse

Absence

The absence of you
Taught me how to deal
With the absence in me
　　　　　—Finally

Lost The Baby (intentional)

For me, you were the fourth trumpet
A violent destruction of my love
One that spun
Then disappeared counterclockwise

For me, you are an empty frame
One I show no one
A treasure in a drawer next to my bed
That holds false memories of three

For her, you were the death of principles
Little eyes that never blinked
But judge her in the mirror the same
The ocean tide, the birth of shame

For us, you were a supernova
A million degrees of inevitable separation
Diagnosed yet never delivered
Pre-linguistic communication

You were the untying of a cherry stem

Unborn

I'm burying bones
With the medicine man
Behind airport bars
While you are planting orchards
With priests
As if that'll put air back in tiny lungs
I'm embarrassed for the spring
Because of its naivety
And the way sunscreen and chlorine
Now smell of misery
We talk at dinner
We cry during movies
We cope, or don't.
Either way
We are staying afloat

April

Sitting
Rotting
In the face of April
Sitting
Rotting
In front of a carousel

You're gone
It's as loud as Hell

The Boy / The Man

I went to Paris with Florence on my tongue
And snapped glass between my elbows
I bit hard on anchored dreams
To let your scent start settling
I thought of stars and the company they keep
And understood why I spend time
With cynical dreamers like me
It's a pleasant pasture
In my other nightmare
Where the boy begs the man to remember him
And—
      The man begs the boy to shoot satellites
      With red rocket ships
      Instead of wrapping up maturity
      To hand himself as a birthday gift
Rather run,
Run to the west coast
Where the future could be brandy soaked
      Because all of life is born from rum casks
      And aged in a wine stain beneath a staircase
      See son—
If you stay here
Life will be beat into your bones
Until you walk with a limp—
Because it carries a memory of its own

Junkyard Dog

I was bred a junkyard dog
Exposed to a costumed thrashing shark
    A bar room brawl
    Wall paint peeling
Arguments serving popcorn ceiling
    On my plate for dinner
Witnessed a tree stump cat autopsy
From a Vietnam Vet vilified for PTSD
    Fiver finger love
Gave me a reprehensible taste for blood
    I was bred a junkyard dog

War Paint

You tried to castrate my words
Like nothing chaotic
Or passionate could contain a message
Well,
I pull tiny pick locks and pills with images
Of your teeth
From between my ribs

I am revision and division
I am damage and parted seas

The acoustic notes you heard
With too much sound
When your father died
    You were eighteen
    It trampled you
Like a nebula implosion
The beginning of embryonic depression
Happiness. Post-partum—
You proudly walked on glass
And wore that blood like
    WAR PAINT
Mother you tried,
And I am your glowing failure
Of a warrior
Assembled with curated bits of shaved spine
I promise that I forgive you

Bloodlines

Bloodlines
Failure and daffodils
Spring in my fists
Skipping hope to soundtracks
Along train tracks
I can see my memory in the shine
Of that shovel
Once used to bury beauty
I felt your misery
As the horror of your failed romances
Left bruises and names in my mouth
That I still cannot pronounce—
      For this I wanted kids too young
        For this I only trust things
That I can hold—for as long
As I can hold them

Promnestria

My lungs breathe something arrogant
Illogically intolerant of keeping you absent
Ambivalent to the muscle above
Keeping time with such introversion
Counting bubbles in vinegar baths
I pretend. I make friends. I do it again.
My backwards dance to the pumpkin patch
Where I play Promnestria between
The holiday and the hurt
We're not yet flipping candy canes
Turning hooks into hangmen
And exchanging presents for sins
I need to get outside and feel
...FUCK, the oven needs cleaned again

We're All Just Urns

We hold God at a table
With the last left leg a little short
It wobbles like a collection of our faith
And serves its purpose as a frame

We hold warmth in our fingertips
Inside gloves;
In the creases of lovers hands
A palm tree pleat in our loud mouths
Spewing desire over the reality
Of life after Holiday

We hold family in a coin jar
That sits atop the stair
At the bend you take
But never recall being there
It collects more dust than change
Which make sense
                    To me anyways

We hold life inside an urn
And in a newborns blink
The meanings of which we eternalize
Inside our skin with tattoo ink

To Understand Depression

Depression is a capricious lover
*****
I used to admire trees
Without giving blessings to their roots
Now I pull people from the soil
Because I can't help but seek the truth

Eye Vs Eye

You were summer caught in leather
Sticky mouth and sweaty songs
Ecstasy drops in a laser show
My heart followed you down
Until we clutched winter in our palms
Traced track marks like recovering junkies
Wasn't this love?
What went wrong?
Seasonal depression sunk our eyes
And teeth
Into false deities

God was both found and lost
In the eyes of the mirror

The Gentrified Romantics Tale

I've been scratching at my eyeballs
Trying to pull blackbirds out of them
To place those evil twins
Back on the power lines from which I stole them
I'm acid washed and coffee soaked
      Part blue eyed battering ram; part misanthrope
      Optic lenses see the fascination of brilliant lives
      Wandering around territorial giants less careful than I

Something beautiful this way came
Well once,
        ...And I ran away

Now I chop wood and smoke alone
Because a heart once stole is
Nothing more
Than the only heart you own

Across oceans and time zones I pine for fresh air
And destruction because my neurosis always takes me there
I'm a gentrified romantic running on backup power
Gathered from famous authors
Who knew not a word of what they wrote
Give me an envelope
Let me write you something lovely
You'll use it as a bookmark in your husbands Christmas
present
He won't appreciate it
because he bathes with motor oil
But he'll pretend to try
And you'll grin
On your way back to me again

Tilting Pennies

You can't scrub me clean of anything
        God isn't watching
It's like trying
   To soften indentions
        That are still indenting
Or baptizing an Arsonist in gasoline

I'll still light myself on fire
Just to know that there isn't anything
Worth saving
        And to witness the burning

Well—
        I never knew you so well
As when I saw you tilting pennies
Between two fingers
Head bowed over the wishing well
In the shadow of the sun
Ten past noon, with liquor floating your lungs
See son,
Getting reborn hurts like a bitch
It's almost altruistic
        But it isn't.

A noble author is still an addict
The clothes just seem to have a better fit

Whiskey, Medicine, Profanity

Those butterscotch and blue eyed days
Have melted away
Into a scratch in the choir
I've spent nights damning God
For these God Damned devils
In your bloodstream
I've rid countries of tea leaves
In search of mercy

Those tarot card bonfires *almost* warmed me

In the years since
I've learned little of living, though—
A great deal about
Whisky,
      Medicine,
         And Profanity

Funeral

Remember fall 2013, do you?
It left me bruised
It still gives me pause
Everyone spoke in glances
Still framed slow-dances
I recall your funeral
I talked too much
Then I let my face rust
I spoke to the sky
And marked my lungs
Like my father did when he was young
You always thought I was being dramatic
To speak of death

But he's my brother's keeper
I've chambered his whispers in my chest

B . D

Some people are like tears in the sea
Others are like rain in the desert

No Witnesses

I'm a jackal with a medicine cabinet
Peroxide bubbling and hot tub brained
Like sanity is a thread to be snipped
Or a pool to be drained
I tapped into the honey vein
And stayed high enough
To search heaven for you among angels
I smiled for the first time in a while
Something genuine
And on the way down
Saw no witnesses in self-reflection
I began cursing any symbolism
It's been 3 years
And I still see you—
In the mirror;
In our hair
In the hemorrhaged color of my eyes
When I cry

You're the landscape around my tooth rot
That burns during the prayers I speak
In the soiled attempts to forgive myself
For this serpent poetry
That's wilting beneath my feet

Living In A Dead Town

Carry heirlooms along conch lined cosmoses
Misplaced dilation—can you hear it?
There is sugar spilling from under the beach roads
Lustrated love gathers 'round the apple rind
And lubricates the crosswalk
Blaming the left arm for the distance from the right side

There's a steel drum dream
Coming from the blue bird chirping
And it sounds like countries colliding
That's just me on medicine
That's just me on medicine

Reset navigation
The Cantina is cancelled
And we're bleeding
All over again
All over the titans of romance
Caught in between Dia de los Muertos
And the screen written halcyon

Some Days

Some days you are bathroom stall poetry
Some days you are a prophet with a pen
An altruistic author collecting rusty nails
A schizophrenic casually organizing devils
Sometimes you pretend
Sometimes you are him

The Places Lost Inside Ourselves

You asked how deep
I said grab a shovel; let's see
Meet me
In the view of panicked worms
Somewhere in the middle
Of a Chinese finger trap
Where I'm courting a whisky glass
Between the bullet and the head
A brothers resting place
A mothers love
A fathers salted limb
And the buoyancy it never provided him

I asked you how deep
You said grab a shovel; let's see
Meet me
In the thick vines I moved into at nine
Cradling a liver
Adopted from a sunburnt stranger
Who babied my back
Before I knew the word "crime"
I remember the belt; how it felt
And how my grandparents tried to drown me
In front of more people I never met
Claiming their eyes could forgive
The sunrise for the sunset

Suitcase

My only souvenir is a suitcase

Silicone and pelvic bone
The babysitter taught that class at home
Confusing L's
Standing in front
Of windows and wishing wells

Twenty-Eight and I still take the bait
Newton spoke of the psychical
Not that intangible weight
Oh well,
A lesson gained from parallels

Crushing nest eggs
Preventing future footprints in the ashtray

My only souvenir is a suitcase

Leaking

There's a leak in this place
It's coming from the small space
Beneath the anchored chandelier
And filling this room
With a voice I haven't heard in years,
Or a tone. Something less maybe?
Either way—
It reminds me that nothing is soft
Except innocence
And that's just a reminder of
       A life less lived.
       A love never had.
       Or lost,
       A battle never fought.

Without reservations I bet bits of myself on people
Just to feel failed,
Which makes me think of you
  Oh how my pureness was mislaid
Murder! Great wildfire of mirrored effigy! Murder!
I'm obsessed with ever body that is not my own
I'm drowned and drained
      It all started with the leak in this place

The Fruit Fly

Triumphed your kingdom with butane
I knew you could
Overbearing; overthinking; overheating
Firefly forethought to remove the foreskin
From that place once forsaken
Tragedy matured and metastasized
Before you had the opportunity

> *It thrusted poverty prior to puberty*
> See,

Every morning is a castle to a fruit fly
Some days your skin
Will appear less human
    More mannequin
Remember that the dance
Will never be as important as the dancing

To The Dead Girl (a pack of smokes)

To the dead girl
You tasted like famine
Nectar soured in a ventricle
Under the pressure of ugly organs
You were a pack of smokes too late
Honey, sea salt, and lemon eyes
It's not your fault
—You were in love
The way a body falls in love with Chemo
Becoming a delicate discipleship
The smallest echo of an actor's heart
I
Made
Love
To
The hardest parts of you
To the indecencies and the mysteries
With a shaved spine
This anemic love left me weightless
And partially blind
No one else seems quite as alive

To the dead girl
You were a pack of smokes too late

Two Fingers

Stage hands feel around
And pull micro expressions
From my pseudo sympathetic aesthetic
Placing asthma in every mourning mouth

Poetry gives trophies to the heartbroken
"Well done, you're really getting fine"
I murdered every nursery rhyme
    And made you eat it.
Eat more of it!
(This digestion is communion)
Then it's bubbling bile that you bring up
With the same two fingers that make you moan

We're all two sides
(And more actually)
Immersed in sanctuaries of habit

Writing About Love Is Only Possible With Open Appendages

Sugar scraped synagogue and
Synesthesia induced from angel winged music
You felt cocaine love
Like your appreciation of it and other drugs
Sun spread toast and caffeine syntax
Breaking like waves through shaky lungs
Quilted metaphors coated that belligerent tongue
Boomeranging to the cigar box
Where I left my heart on damaged lips
With lingering smoke in casino bedrooms

Could I put you in a syringe
Play Sinatra on vinyl
And lay veins on a skeleton?

Morning heat bounces off of the complex
And complexes
Shared between two mental mansions
Housed inside of physical attraction
Like writing about love was only possible
With our appendages

Our benevolence was born with an asterisk
Which we erased with a first kiss

Like A Forgery

She said
I curse too much
And don't laugh enough
But
I fuck like I write

So she stayed
Until I began to make love
Then left like steam

With our life still authored
In my sheets
I feel that
           I just fuck like a forgery

Symmetry To Being Lonely

Everything became slow
The way stains formed
From blinks
To how bruises grow
The vinyl spins
My spine softens
I get drunk and read old poetry
I swear there's some symmetry
To being lonely
It's not love I regret
It's retaliation I guess

And how my liver kept your name
Because it drinks for you

Expose for me
Your tattered tendencies
We all have scars
We just wear them differently

Separate Homes

I gave you salt stitches
Like some drunken magician
And cried out to you at 3 am
Darling, "You are enough"

I'm intelligently written
Emotionally stricken
Honestly, I'm a liar
But I work hard at it

Don't forget the note on the fridge
Or to check the tread on your tires

There's a heart on your wrist
I know you'll study
And stare at it
Long after the separate homes
We've settled in
Until it begins to fade
And you'll sit up and say

"I knew all along
You wouldn't stay"

Glass Monuments

Saline reduction between the bars
And blinds of homes we wake up in
But don't belong to.

A photographer's daughter
Told me once—that adoration
Is building a mountain to a blind man
Alas, the height of Absolution.

Termites tap sap from the tree
And trick me
Tempting my hormones to play cruel
You're tipsy before you're gutted
And I was worn cheese cloth thin
From my crusade
The morning after reconciliation

Knighthood possessed,
Strewn about the purring animals
Like I was conducting a miracle,
As if I could
Be a medicine or a cure—either or,
The bridge burns and you choose a side
Or bob silver like a bellied fish
Becoming the cracks even Gods fingers miss

Pugilist / Poet

I panic in the light
Because everyone can see my dark
My hearts a utility
And my shame is similar in necessity

Soak the encore of this pugilist
In his sad analogy
Collect all the blood
And call it poetry

Dislocating Love

Coat hangers and thumbtacks
Injuring and indenting index fingerprints
Remind me of confronting my rumination

(GO AHEAD:
Hang me on the same wall that theory was framed on)

I was an orphan in Varsity sweats
Dusting blood brother droplets
Off the furniture of a house never lived in
While adopting to strong bones
Practiced to stand through cyclical sadness
I am now made of soil covering an ancient burial ground
Over bodies of barrel battled westerners
Not yet found

Hurricane winds and the household goods
Lost in them
I am those tangible memories
And the acceptance of how little they matter

Rejuvenation; an old sea brigade
Firing cannons at sorority sins
And the mechanical men
Dislocating love just for a taste of them

The Rope In The Attic

The muscles in my neck spasm
I guess they always have
In the presence of that end table
At the thought
Of third grade soft skull shots
A reflection of your love for potential
But never the body that housed it
      Unless you were a masochist
Full of hoppy blood
And self-hate
      But I don't judge

Thanksgiving grieving through prayer hands
Became normal
      While the rope in the attic still hung
And fostered smiles floated atop the gravy
      While the rope in the attic still hung
And Christmas was paid for with guilt
      While the rope in the attic still hung

The Ocean Still Gives Me You

I recall my bubblegum days
When you were still alive
Before that sticky memory
Became bulimic mornings
And I gave my liver your name
It's preserved—
Like Vienna Sausage lunches
And punk rock dreams
Of seeing Dublin
Before our letter jackets and stolen booze
Became rings and wedding suits.

I can still see your face
As we spit at ships docked in the bay
Knowing if we missed
Parts of us were eternalized
In the ocean waves
                    Every now and then
                    I find the water
                    And swim
                    So I can feel close to you again.

Remembrance

It was a picture of
A widow at a gravestone
Waiting
Hours after the eulogy
That brought you back to me
In my A.M thoughts
I remember you
Like I remember sobriety
Or that medical bracelet
They made me wear for three days.

Father's Day (dementia)

Rusty pipes leaving water spots above my eyes
Fangs ripping through memories
Of theme parks, 10 fingers and whisky
How about today,
Do you remember me?
My face is rippled water
On a garage door painting
Can I pull each tooth, and sell the root
For another hour where your mind stays?

Cigarettes never took your lungs
The war didn't take your brain.

You're the 5.4 million Americans
Searching for their own name

        NO

I won't downsize you to a fucking ribbon
And put your legacy on my chest in some parade
Happy Father's Day

Reminders

I hate how we became
Bloodless
Bad steps
Consoling marriages
On a park bench
(a pigeon feeder with a knit cap)

A reminder
Of a time back when
We could have been
Gold thieves on an endless cloud stretch
Of bar brokers and blue sea steps

An ancient idea of love
Where Zeus would have blessed us
And calligraphy pens
Carved from unicorn horns
Would ink our vows

Prologue

There are things about the last time we saw each other that I pushed gently into the flood. The water drained after a few months and took all those soppy little remnants that used to make me believe in things like serendipity. I don't anymore. Believe in serendipity that is. I took control when that flood came and finally understood why our bodies are made from so much water.

A month from now; a year from now; a decade from now someone will find those pieces. They'll dry them off and learn to love them much like I did. Maybe this time you'll exist like a pillow between its casings. Or a bookmark. I hope so. I don't wish anything bad towards you. You weren't a vulture or an animal. You didn't attempt to maul my lungs so I couldn't speak. Moving on was the easiest thing. You made it so. Which is actually, now that I think about it, the most difficult thing to swallow.

Somewhere across the country, the coast and two oceans, you're still thinking about me. A book in hand and probably one of those horrid smoothies. There will still be that bit of dust lining the piano that never got cleaned. I'm sure my dead skin cells are still there, resting and watching over you.

We're all lingering, or allowing things to linger inside of us.

I Named Four Children

I've been laughing all night
With the children of mine
The ones that never blinked their eyes
I wasn't supposed to bend
But beauty will cut you like a tree
       Sometimes
And sleep won't fix a thing
Maybe provide a flavored dream
The citrus will linger
On your half of the bed
That I burnt your ghost in
      I guess really—
Some things should be forgotten

Racing White Rabbits

Beach side sedations with a coconut in my fist
To escape counting size five ring fingerprints
Left on the screen door
Oil and biology
But I pretend them to be
A gift your ghost left me

I'm racing white rabbits
Both day and night
The faucet leaks
The laundry sits in clumps
Like aging skin, and
The faucet leaks
My mind is oscillating
And the dog won't yet sleep
On your side of the bed

Truth / Pain / Hope

Truth is stale bread
It is sour milk
And Christmas in a bottle

Pain is an ornament
Pulled from an attic box
Once a year

Hope is the wine stain you ignore
By choice
Because you like the tablecloth more

You are a kill shot
Red sand and two names
In the past I was you
In the future, you are me
Do you see?

Hallways

Long lungless lunges
Down bubblegum hallways
Where the volume of your voice
Hasn't stopped echoing

That poorly patched place in the wall
Where you finally understood
The alchemy of my passion
Would outmatch your violence
Is still conspicuous

And

I'd trade this dissonance
In—
          For cigarette burns and decaf coffee
I'm already addicted to my own impatience
And

Every night I polish the scissors
I used to cut our ties

Sick

I got sick again
Trapped on the 13th floor
Rotten as an apple
That doesn't know the tree it fell from
                    So I fell in love with history
                    Because I didn't know my own
Everything smells like lidocaine

Well..

They don't allow whisky eyes to observe shame here
I think about how you kissed
I think about how you put me here
Without meaning it
Somedays I talk about it
Most days I don't
Most days I'm cold and self-indulgent
I can't pretend
I feel sick again

Half(ed)

Anchored to your ankles was a chain
Images of pickled poses,
Rose` holidays, and—
Black beach memories
You were somewhere in the pebbles
    Handsome and short
Beauty was bought in the flower shop
Prior to speaking other languages

Now fluent in behavior
You see we actually spin history in reverse

Oh boy, you'll become
Something to revere
But for now feelings are nothing to fear
You're spear hunting in strong current
Shedding tomorrow to have a little extra today
With restless legs
You grow like shoots and stalks
And those cradled thoughts
Will always be grateful
For the museum view from the mausoleum
That you shoved your love in

Those little menagerie hearts you kept
Polished,
With a healthy dose of placement and truth
Half-drunk, half-promised, half-purposed
Half, just half
Like life and pronoun(ed) tattoos
Wet wheeled and clunked grey inside of
Casket contrast
Tie it with ribbons
And be free

The festivity of the gravedigger
Is the flattery of the swan song
Inviting old age like wine
We are nothing, if not lessons in light
The yin and yang of the heart does exist
Trust me, I found it
In scotch and tradition
In the memory of kids
Present, past, and never had
It does exist
In the embrace of a lovers wish
To be a home to walk the day into midnight
with

I Exist In Moments Of Wet Paint

I carve flowers in your name
Watch the petals fall
Like wet paint on the page
Our love was a western
6-shooter, 12 paces
One with fame
The other,
Left with empty vases
I drowned the hairdryer you left
Nothing, I felt nothing
You were dresses and dopamine
Immeasurable beauty
With a heart of coal

NOW

I am a man of many
Many rooms with several mirrors
Compartmentalized
Conceptualized
Nail bit, gear shifted
Noah changed history
And let all board his ark

All except for me

So I exist in the moments of wet paint
Right before the permanent you
Takes place

THE THINGS THAT WE KEEP
CHAPTER TWO

You Gave Me More Than You Know

I found strength on the shoulders of dead friends
But,
When I met you, love made sense
It felt like freedom
And why people stand in the sunshine
It felt like redemption
I never told you what kissing those soup can scars
On my thigh did
But,
It felt like they never happened
Like I dodged a bullet
I felt lifted
It felt like something bigger than God existed

How We Fell In Love

We fell in love over the hum of intellectuals
Nested between the fangs of wolves
We searched the depths of mason jars
After the knell of summer nights
        That liquid warmed our stomachs
While watering gardens we'd barely acknowledge
Goddammit though, we internalized it

We shared ghost stories from lives forgotten
Exorcised demons over menthol smiles
And with pressed lips
Realized we were no longer haunted

Not by iron fists
Not by childhood rebellion
Not by morals missile'd at the steam-engine

Somehow, those glossy eyed snow angels
Returned to us
Full of grade school purity and trust

Though I sexualize your body,
It's the integrity of your heart that I lust

True Scale Of Love

I am the stolen reflection of an unveiled heart
The sound of octaves climbing
Like the true scale of love was written
With my non-dominant hand
And that's why I was never able
To understand
Until now
Until you.

Wedding Vow

I've written words for burn victims
For the death stricken
For the heart broken (organ donors)
I've written words that I've meant
And some that I didn't
My pen has settled in milk and in oil
It's created more bone than God
I've written simple notes
That expired after morning coffee
I've written about timelessness
And how we hear eternal music
From a caged canary
Just to free the bird,
And title it temporary
I've written so much
But nothing more important
As these words true
I shall never want a me without a you
I Do
My love, I Do

The Places You Become Poetry

The lungs of cowboys are displayed in museums
And nobody smokes anymore
Instead we sleep in graffiti boats
Already anchored to the ocean floor

The thesis is my own fragmented condition
Shaken in Panko crumbs
Sleeping in the unfed mouths
Of those still wetting our thumbs

And we are all, wet.
Behind the ears,
And in the places we didn't learn about
Until we were dry enough to understand
It's normal though—
For the ocean to teach the whale
About its heritage bones
Buried in some desert sand.

But I digress into a cluttered dichotomy
Between con and confidence,
Where we create symphonies
And in the breathing room—
That's where you become poetry

Please Haunt Me

Please haunt me
Through memoirs and memories
The thin pages of authored dreams

Please haunt me,
In flame colored walls
Of cities I haven't seen sunrises in yet
Through songs along coastlines
In the passenger seat
As white caps resemble teeth

Please haunt me,
In thirty-dollar hotel room bible drawers
And the blessings from the mother you met
But will never meet

Please haunt me,
Between the mirror and the drummers tap
Riddled middle finger thoughts
And pungent graphite mental prison trap
Lovely ghost
Grave inside my grieving bones
Lift my dreams
—Please haunt me

I Want To Bring You Back To Life

I want to taste the wild. I want to taste wild.
I want to hide myself between ten fingers
of night and belong. Belong to wet rocks
and hot coals. I rake myself over history
and eat winter during each season, for I have
good reason. I want to plant myself in dead
gardens; the kind that exist in disloyal and
lackluster lovers trying to make up for their
stolen valor. I want to bring you back to life.

My Remnants

I could paint you a picture of my ribcage
Ivory and blood arranged like a floral landscape
You'd hang it on the refrigerator for a moment
Just to replace it during your next cigarette break
See—
          I lost love before I even knew what it was

That's why I only understand happiness
When I'm chasing it

          If they handed out trophy's for damage
          I'd have to buy a separate place
          Just to house them in

Sometimes in the dark I try to taste it
The stale perfume
The dollar store fingernail polish
The Government cheese sandwiches

          These are my remnants of sadness

Why warmth is a bird seen through bars of a prison
In my heart it can never be spring
Because your memory is ever lingering

Do Not Read This

Do not read this:

It's of failure and feathers
Whirl-winding in a storm
Of licorice and chewing gum
I listened to my heart for the first time
When I saw my father cry

It staples to the inside eye lid

The kind of memory that begs you to listen
When you devour pizza at one a.m
Or watch sprinklers run too long
Or count your ribs under covers
Of French pressed sheets
With military corners tucked too tightly

It's of vacuum sealed shirts
And Republican conversations
Roasting under noon flights, fishing for silence
It caught us—I saw it again
A hernia burst and you've never looked so calm
A patchwork of bravery, and I began
To finally understand
Why the snare tap slows one fourth beat
It's for times like these
That we surrender just to keep

Do not read this:
You will not find those brilliant metaphors
You may be looking for
Father, you are the strength of the storm
And this is from where my conviction was born

People Like We

People like me, we—
Are vaccinated artifacts
Clinging to cursory ideologies
Written in cursive with the left hand
Not to be excavated
Or translated properly

People like me, we—
Smell like gin and diner food
With bones holding the secrets to
True art & true love,
Shall our bodies ever be exhumed

People like me, we—
Are crafted from ink and coffee
Measured by the carafe
Finding meaning like a gentle colony of bees
Neurotic and stressing over forgotten beliefs
Like loyalty

Stay strong people like we
Those who don't understand
Will try to steal you away from me

A B a c k T h e n

Memories formed inside of codeine cocktails
Existing in some kind of collapse
While building tomorrow's
Out of sunlight and laughter
Then it happened
Like water bugs; the scatter

Auditorium ears assembled like
Matchsticks in a box
Daisy drawn eyelids
Like mornings were meant
For more than just breakfast

It contained promise
What is promise?

Twenty nine and there are families and kids
Adopting sequels to our genetic sins

I missed the siren call—
I'm still drunk off of pinky swears
And dinner at 3am
Left wondering if
There was ever beauty in "back then"
Because we settled in
Suits of people that forgot
There ever was a "back then"

The People We Meet

Some people we meet
Because they are meant to show
Not how far we have come,
But how far we have left to go

Someone Like Me

My honor has always rested
On the tip of my pen
Felt stamped in the blood bank
Where I was reborn
Change sometimes takes a new kidney
Something auxiliary;
Fireproof hands surrendering to a lobotomy

The moon and I have some chatting to do
About Walden Pond
And how Halloween is beautiful in a way
That only monsters understand

It took two trips around the world
With the company of leather hands
To uncover the difference between
Why we see people in things
And people as things

The heart has a wedding ring sanctity
But the soul hates trading youth
For the futurity of preserved loyalty

That fear removes the integrity from humanity

      I guess that's why it took so long
      To find someone like me

B . N . H

I think my veins itch
Or yearn
Or beg
Something valued, consumed,
And got lost in them
It was me
It was you
Dark eyes
And disorders you don't talk about
In specific order
Anyways
I want to promise you things
And be so present
That you forget the word
Abandonment
I know you feel so full
Inside cathedrals
Despite the fact that you don't believe
In God
I ache to let you know
You are value
And you are valued

I Try To Belong To Unrequited Love

I've done some healing
But age gathers in my cheeks
It spoils to a hymnal
That I memorized a long time ago
And disposed of somewhere inside of me
Flaunting itself to my hip bones
To my clavicle and
Through my ear canal, gaudily
   This echo has me blushing—

I try to belong to unrequited love
For a father that's been missing,

But wind up chewing craters
With my soft teeth
Remembering and repeating
Remembering and repeating
I made a hell for myself
In the heaven
   That it has been neighboring

Lioness

I dip my fingers into crevices
   —Yours
During warm picnics
Apricot and butterscotch
Soak into my soil
And I bloom
Losing touch with loneliness,
With gravity, with darkness

My lioness,
I've been living again
Inside of your mouth
Resting easy between
Your mild tusks
Though I feel your need to eat
I'm still alive
Even after pulling on your tongue
Several times
       Let me be your offering
Somewhere between
The lip, the hip, and the spine
There's a miracle
Like a continent
I claim it as your octaves climb

Measure The Earth

I want to measure the earth with you
Using only our footprints

We may never get our mouths wet
At the fountain of youth

But you'll always be as beautiful
As the day we first met

Too Much Of Anything

Just because you love the rain
Doesn't mean you can't drown

Fast Food Wrappers

Fucking fast food wrappers.
The smell of permission and potential expiring.
It's dead. Everything is dead.
White etcetera's
Tweaking militias with malaria
Watching emerging markets
Flow from greedy noses
Drunken parents swinging at past selves
I must have looked like him. Or her.
Their good deeds died too
In the explosion of that seed.
It's all dead I said!
Not in the head, but in the heart
We all die there first.
Drowning in the loss of something we thought we owned
Like people, or beach front homes.

One cannot have the tide
For it keeps and releases at the same time
We can't even own ourselves.
Not until we're soaked in guilt
And buried in fucking fast food wrappers

Grandma

Soft eggs remind me of longing
Like wine at noon
Or airport departure gates
A place hearts go to congregate

My Grandmother died
Before my fifth birthday
                    of heartache
That taught me one thing—

Love will kill you if you let it
Which is familiar,
Because Bukowski
Said to find it
...Goddamn that woman was a romantic

Sunday Poetry

There are things that drip away
And others that just stay

Like Sunday poetry

A hymn in a hammock
To which,
We swore to live without memories
Eternal sunshine
And a broken crystal ball
Anything less
And someday
We'll become nothing at all

Time And Place

There is a time and place for orphaned poetry
For saltine dinners and tomato soup dresses
While the bluebells are spinning in sunflowers
For the sun tanned wedding bands
In the front row

Yes
There is a time for pinpricked romantics
Biting their tongues to a kettle song
Lifting their willowed hands
Just to write it down wrong

There is a time for lace underwear
And new beds
And animals at the feet of them
For splitting lady luck
In a nine bedroom beach home with jello shots
To trade fears for future weather

There is a time for all these things
For baby-breath apologies;
For bar stool eulogies;
For Chicago bound finder feeds;
But now—
Now is not the time for me

Bloodthirsty

My poetry walks like the Old Testament
—It is bloodthirsty—
Dyed in the wetness of time
I uncovered naked warriors of myself
And raised them with a pack of wolves
I named each of my teeth
Casanova—
My grandiloquence will lull you to sleep
In the mouth of an assassin
While I burn all weedy rhetoric
Until its absence is prehistoric

On day one
I quelled infinity in lace
With thumbs pressed to the earth
Searching for a taste
Joining the lonely lovers
Carving heart out of the city streets
As if all the worlds romantics
Stripped themselves of summer
To comprehend gravities discipline
And the hourglass shape of opinion

Oh, Glory be bound to those brave enough to seek it
Oh, Love be bound to those brave enough to keep it

The Killing

It was the smell of watermelon
And innocence melting
As summer squeezed his life into a truck bed
With all of his belongings
California had pupils the size of revolver barrels
And anger popping like grape seeds
    —Goddammit they better stay there

I wrote it in bold colors
Like that meant something
As if the plums beneath your hospital gown
Which turned into scars and loss of religion
Could be absolved by a man
And his distance

Two months, fast-forward
Snow drifts brought back the cobra coiled
A disposable genius gaining a peephole interest
But I was a hawk
  Circling his dashboard
    —He twitched like vacation storm hands
Then relaxed
Guilt is a dress worn by a cheating bride
Not I;
This was for her protection
    —I sleep like a justified Darwinian

My Amen

You are of things
Like pirate ships
And Saturn's rings

Tannin dreams
Among amateur pallets
A dog whistle frequency

My rose
In an Atlantis adjacent garden

You are mythology;
You are adrenaline;
You are Amen

Of Love Or Beauty

I've seen beauty, for—
I've watched a sunrise bend Greece at its knees
Lovers chased their white wine with coffee
And the simplicity tempted me

I've tasted beauty, for—
I've sipped Champagne with serendipity
As she carried passengers in paper planes
Across the Baltic Sea
I swear,
Their vows made honey less sweet

I've felt beauty, for—
It sprinted through me
Atop Korea where the wind seeks matrimony
To anything
In fact, it was the first time I understood spirituality

Then I saw you
And realized I knew absolutely nothing of
Love or beauty

Fetish

She was the softer colors
The kind that cling to the edges
Bondage without the chains
It felt religious in a way
To worship footsteps
Because they walked with grace
And commanded me
I've never understood this kind of fetish
Until it was her feet telling me which way to go

She

She is a brilliant tapestry of triangles
An angelic shape
That turned boys into impatient men
She even made Ireland blush
IN FACT
After drawing her face from a constellation
Apollo surrendered his pen
Knowing not a single more beautiful thing
Could ever be drawn or written

You Belong Here

Some people
Want to give you the world
I would rather make you feel
Like you belong in it

My Favorite Splinter

You are dry cinnamon in my wet mouth
Still eyed and smoke knotting your tongue
I kissed your pulse to untie the heartbreak
To bring your father back
From the patriot of some lost song

We were a concussion kiss
Something that obliterated all that came
Before this

Lovers lie and lovers lay
Though we argue on topics like
The loyalty of its weight
I'm asking you to stay

Shall we become another verse
To one of my miserable poems
I'll use it to warm my hands during future winters
I'll stay a graceless writer
You'll forever be, my favorite splinter

Christmas

Hope is an aphrodisiac
Cooking sugar
Like carols on Christmas
In the shadow of my buried
Orestes Complex
We won't reminisce your sins
As long as we're trading budget
For pine scents and ornaments

The Proclamation

We must learn to be <u>more</u>
Than waiting room promises
Made at the Feet
Of a God
That we ignore

Wild Love

Break in two
Let the brooding button ups in coffee shops
Hold their heartbreak in warm hands

We nurse fragile time at daybreak
And at midnight
Begging for metamorphosis
During moonlit kisses

A silent scribble can't bring back
A moment—
Or expand upon it
So let's find beauty in violent silence
Keep it in our chest

Our inevitable separate graves
Can bloom with wildflowers
So all of our tenses
Remind them of our wild love
And existence

The Beautiful Truth

On your angular descent from the moon
You landed among men
Somehow—I was one of them
I loved you in two ways
    Fistful of roses
    Fistful of prayer
Legends were sent here
And I didn't belong;
Not to them.

I belong to you

    I've never accepted <u>a more beautiful truth</u>

Birthday Letters

I left you alone to eat your demons
Oh, unsympathetic surgeon I am
Am I?
You were listening to Dandelion Wine
I always said it was my favorite song
Some days, some days
Some days—before the lean in language
Before I understood Ted Hughes
Before crushes became crushing

We're all pretty string instruments and gasoline
Offering cheers to casino love

I bet it all—
Along crushed roses and beach roads
My mouth slurs and slides
Etching all you loved, into the sides
Of sand dunes with seashells

There was an endless sense of sound
Under a billion stars
And I became a half-written letter
Stamped into the Universe with you

Indelible

Indelible
Chewing your memory
With hearts
Still layering my teeth
Squeezing love like a balloon
Or beating it
Like a piñata
Until something inevitable happens
Like distance
   Like hope
      Like survival

I can't replace you
I wouldn't want to

The Hero To My Story Is You

You're my little bit of magic
And madness
In this world too fixated on future islands

Your name is mellifluous
Such a gentle drug
You keep me from feeling lonely
Or like anything other than me

You are my only promise in this world
Full of decoration
A beautiful imbue

Darling, the hero to my story
Will always be you

Resilient Love

The proof of love is equal only
To the power over your heart
That you offer to another

I hope you know though I curse these oceans
I believe in a love that is resilient
I believe that we are built different

Rules

There are rules
Trust me
Some are golden
Some are irrevocably relevant

They are poetry, see—
I would brave the winds of plague
And
Play piano with the teeth
Of famous men
Just to bury all of that
And place a promise on your partner finger
Engraved with the single most important
Three words ever written

Darling, there are rules
Arabica soaked and witnessed
On stones held atop some mountain
And I will abide by them

Not because I'm a fool not to
But because I realize I'm a fool without you

The Weight Of Gold

Her heart made every room lighter
Though it weighed a thousand pounds
        Of pure gold

I Can't Stop Bleeding

Little triggers
They're Jurassic, actually.
Coffee at 7:05
I'm five minutes behind
Drop everything today
It's all fragile anyways
So it seems.
Why are my feet bleeding?
Cleaning the glass wasn't scheduled.
She gets me. Like, really—but,
She hates the sight of blood
And I can't stop fucking bleeding
On top of barstools
On pages in coffee shops
The words must mean something
They have to mean something
And she must really love me
Because I can't stop emptying
I only hope she knows
That I do it
To make more room for her

B e

Be vicious. Be proud. Be proper. But only when it counts. Be your own savior. At times, allow yourself to care enough to save someone else. Be brave. Brave enough to empty out and start again. Have enough perspective to see both sides of the coin. Be a vacation unto yourself in a space that you call your own. Write in cursive because we don't anymore. Let everyone curse you because they can't understand. Let them be them. Be what matters. Be you.

A Meal With A Black Widow

I watched the sun rise
With a black widow dining
I thought of all the people I've eaten
And those that consumed me

I remember life without energy drinks
One with poodle skirts and chivalry
When did the razor's edge tip?
Did Occam and Murphy share some whisky
On the day they got it all right?
I like to believe that's why I drink
       See—

It was Hemmingway and Bukowski
That taught me how to be a true romantic

       Be so realistically ugly
       That the truth becomes illuminating

Aging Addictions

Aging addictions
Molding fangs from wax
And hanging droplets of youth
From my lapel
Cardinals on the neighborhood cathedral
Carry rainy teeth
And it got me

Like sunsets in Greece
Athens chewed and chewed
Until my commute was coffee
                              And nicotine

A neoprene scent carried my personality
In a shallow sheath
And I wrote about you
Clinging to virtues of love in my sheets
And the rules of pain embedded in our
Now stored bedding

It's all poetry
It's what separates "us" from "we"
It's all poetry

Pay Attention

Earnest like hangover regret
Or a hand me down appendectomy
Addicted to shuffling cutlery
Shifting from you through—
My knowledge of cytometry

Now, adjusting my plot in the cemetery

I'm chrome and casein
Whisky and words
All wasted on love drunk anarchists
Singing caffeine songs to Eve about Adam
Expecting pure pollination from pollution

When you're 40 and in church
Because you needed a man to believe in
I'll say
You should've paid more fucking attention

Echo

I thought you'd be quick like a bee sting
At most a sunburn
You turned out to be, more third degree
A psychiatric ward symphony
With no way out, the sound never really leaves

It wasn't attempted suicide
It was a botched surgery
I just wanted to remove the worst parts of me

How About Then?

What if I drank less?
Quit gambling with my sadness

How about then?

I could learn to swallow circus swords
And juggle fire torches
Or start a company and buy an island

If I did, would you consider it?

What if I cut my hair?
Go to church
And talk less to things that aren't there?

I'll acknowledge my faults, I swear.
I can read your favorite books,
Sleep more,
And buy a birdfeeder in sight
From our porch swing
I can talk about the future
And stock up on candles and flashlights

What about then?

Could we bury our missed opportunity
In the backyard?

Mess

I'm a manicured mess
You're a calculated corpse
Disrobed, we're both
Star spangled dreamers
Removing stitches
To fall in love
    With falling in love

Love Is Often A Hologram

Let me hit the oxygen
Smoking out from that boom box generation
I'll trace those petals that fell
As chaos melted on your wrist

Mediocre eyes will pry
If only we could've framed that moment
The one where you emptied the skies
As if the stars weren't pure enough
To be judged by the symmetry of our souls
Colliding,

I'll keep writing
About the rogue lizard tongues
The ones with jaws drawn
And morals like migratory birds
Oh, they will try to poach you
Though I've drank the loyalty from your lips
I'll always admit
That I'm fearful of this

Love is often a hologram—
Watching the direction of our feet
Surrendering to this adrenaline coursing
Is my way of admitting
That I have something important to keep

Tether

That stare—
It traveled to my gut
Like Houdini's punch
I became
A beggar who struck the lottery
Lost it all,
And can't remember life without money
In this world of floating balloons
You gave me a welcomed tether
And while everyone else
Is following the map
Searching for treasure
We're sitting back
Laughing,
Because we already found it

Serendipity Of Old Souls

My soul sits with the Castle of Sirmione
An old romantic
Preserved perfectly and left strategically
In the 13th Century
Strangers have entered
Some have taken parts of me
But not one stayed
            They were all too ordinary
I never let beauty be devouring
An aesthetic door still serves its purpose
Ever swinging.

All these guests;
All these aged haunts
Left me an asthmatic with cigarettes
I thought my love must be preserved too
Somewhere in a wine cellar
Held captive by a collector

In my dreams she was dust blowing my way
Settling on wildflowers and bottles
Floating atop the wakes made in the bay

Then all at once she arrived
Like a shadow I felt her presence
The familiar kind; the calming kind
And old souls we were
Young at heart, and right on time

Hold Time

I wish that I
Could hold time
The way that
I hold you

The Original Symphony

You are the original symphony
Megaphone diary
Playing deep inside of me
Pictures of angel wings
Doing nothing but orbiting
Constantly
You are a tip toe 360
Both dizzying and mystifying
I find wine on your tongue
And sunsets between your teeth
How did I get this lucky?
I certainly don't deserve any honey
But this truth is lacquered between my palms
cementing my promise four rows down
    And hung on the fridge now
I feel happy
I didn't think I walked the stairs
That led me to this kind of history
But I believe, I believe, I believe,
That love made me wise
Darling—
Home is a miracle I found in your eyes

Two Birds

I look at you differently
Like something that's never
Been held properly
Darling, We
Are two birds in a nest
Both bound and free

Weathervane

I'm your weathervane
Depend on me
And I'll release the rain into the sea
So we can see the difference between
What matters
And what just flirts with love
Sometimes all it takes is a little shove

You smoke too many cigarettes
Like your lungs are trying to find company
And your fingers are needy blessings
Extending from some heroine
That may have given birth to Mother Mary
In a previous life

You smile at the broken ones
Because it gives you purpose
And that makes you sad
Because you're using all those tears
On other drowning plants

I can tell that

By the cracks in your hands
I want to soften them like your eyes
So that one day
You'll have faith in a vase
Not for the flower you admire
But for the reflection of time

Two Lovers Trapped In An Asylum

I've always been
Two lovers trapped
In an asylum
Pastels drifting
Along neon mornings
(Christmas in the limbic system)
You brought symmetry
Offered absolution
To every ugly memory
And now I finally see
The best part of everything

You're standing right in front of me

Setting Forest Fires

I don't want to waste the weather
It's perfect for body snatchers
And waking up with scars I can't admit to
I'm adhering my admiration
To the way you have me
Swallowing salamanders
Aiming arrows at bullseyes, drunkenly;
Performing root canals on the dead
(Wait, what was just said?)
Well—
I soaked all the branches in gasoline
And watched the sunrise burn our forest clean

Sequel To Nervous Light

You are the sequel to nervous light
The kind of sunrise
That sets the carpet on fire
And makes me count breaths
I was nothing but a runaway
A temporary child
With a distrust for perfume
And, well—
Anyone like you

My bones are an orphanage
I'm all amphetamines and smoke
Drowning in the fluorescents
Of your confident glow
⠀⠀⠀⠀⠀⠀I talk like a lush
⠀⠀⠀⠀⠀⠀I need to believe
That together we'll always speak
Like a couple of moonlit drunks

Significant

You will grow to miss
The things you find insignificant
The linear value of beauty
Is held <u>not</u> in a single moment

ALL OTHER THINGS
CHAPTER THREE

The New Century Of Love

There is a century of love
Balled up and balanced inside my fists
The marrow of some hipster stranger
Has been sucked dry, by—
The dopamine addiction
And replaced with the face of Jesus Christ
Tattooed on the thigh

(You think you love like religion
Really you just kiss like the devil)

Limerence has become a pathological right
Fucked into our craft beer generation

We promise potential just to eat an extra portion
Of this, or that—
Or her and him
Hymens tear to the tune of rotational affection
And cock-strong frat boys are praised
For passing stories of quantity to carriage kids

Alcohol reflections lick our shins
But that's how "we" cleanse
Society became—
                    Only as loyal as its options

To Return, You Must Leave

I burnt my lungs
As I drug myself down the Kingdom
Of Thailand
And lived lipless between the legs
Of a vindictive past
Memories are sometimes like that

I begged my friends
To pity the country I've become
And try to love my new hues
Isolated like the Northern Blues

A sailboat soul in El Dorado
With a T-shirt on
Clover clutched and soul spent
On such promiscuous promises
My age went backward and forward
In the bath water wave
Then emerged emancipated from your pain
Finally—
I've always huddled it between
My shoulder blades

Red feathered heart and passion crossed
The East coast spoke to me
Through time zones
In a language once heard
But never understood

In the folds of time
I fathered a ghost
And found truth on the third ring
Of Saturn
In a foreign dream pressed 'neath
The Oak Wood

Reality

Sticky
It drips and dries
Clings to the bones
Like Plath or Bronte
Forces you
To appreciate the pain
In a way
That feels like love
  Ruined sculptor
  Attacks and atones
Sugar cubes on horses tongues
Like breasts below plastic collar bones
Continents exists between fictional legs
They give wishes
A better place to die

Grotesque
I reiterate
Then regenerate
Like a Polaroid of Russian nesting dolls
Love yourself
Or love them all
Then take your hangover to bed
Reality is a fantasy assembled in your head

The Dream

Smoke bomb the ferry
The mystery was lost in the collapse
A jugular shot from the biker gang
Throwing fists in my mental library

I woke up on the other side of the sun
In a stash house
By the Hollywood Hillside pool
Next to Bloody Mary Death March survivors
Looking for quills and ink jugs

These theologians had Gemini eyes
They studied pornography
And Greek Mythology the same
While huddled around ashtrays
Poaching cherries with their vernacular
And using first editions as plates

I returned home like a footprint in dry sand
The way you can only feel a dream
Hours after you wake
Maybe nothing happened the way I explained
But I'll never be the same

Who Taught You To Be You

I've been told that I have a nervous twitch
A tell of sorts
When my speech rate increases
And the hearts in the room can't keep up
Because they've been dependent
On antidepressants
...since Greek Mythologist's suggested
The tinier the phallic symbol
The more intelligence he expressed

You've all been shelled in the belief
That a goddess walks at 5 foot 9 with a large...
(Well since then, you've all been falling behind)
Reading all the "Classics"
Because you never really understood Mark Twain
He said it's something we all know exists
But never actually read,
Essentially it's a provocative frame

I talk too much
Right?
I should be rawer and more vulgar
Because Bukowski taught you how to feel
When you went Love broke for the first time
Right!?

I should quit with the sharp vestige
And public proclamations in my poetry
It's making everyone uneasy
Make it short and sweet
Some soft soliloquy
Because rebellion ages with grace

Four Letters

Waiting for our love to coagulate
Now stasis: the opposite
Sympathy from my concubine
Safe; only in the word—
Hinged shovel to the wall
Father time has a deal with the reaper
  And the human race
  Keeps trying to outrun the handshake
Einstein was a drunk—
  Or at least an orphan with an orgasm
Foreplay existed in his fourth dimension
Where,
He bore witness to his psychoanalysis
  Love is in the unwanted
  And the unwanted just want it

The Men Forgotten

Good men go home at ten
       The rest stay in the sea weed
       Polishing their false teeth
       Discussing picket fences
       And French Kitchens
       Where secrets keep—
       Until extracted by floss and toothpicks
Great men get their 5'oclock shadows
       Idolized by bomb builders in basements
       Of single mothers
       Who never became their "truest self"
       And by their own affidavits
       Choose metaphors over ascension
       After all,
       Pocket squares are just unnecessary stitches
And the men forgotten?
       Well,
       Those men found love

Sex And Summer

Shape shifted
Like bible school days
Transitioning
To sex and summer
The taste of
Club soda souring
In our parents mouths
We longed for longing
Tying cherry stems
With a type writer innocence
Until there was no more fruit
Left in the garden

To Be Missed

I just want to be missed
Like the scent of the sea
To the desert sun

I just want to be
Your spotty memory
The one that mauls you to sleep
Or begs you awake
Forced to face that empty space,
And lack of shape
Beside you in the bathroom mirror

You're expensive taste baby
Living out cheapened fantasies
Our love is a conversation
Held underwater

I Gave Too Much

I give too much—leaving
Footprints in these dead head clubs
Bank rolling pleasure
With tobacco eyes

A Rembrandt on display
Of the shredded mercury poisoning painting
Still leaking in the corner

I gave too much—grinning
Something stupid still staining my face
Returning applause to that forgotten memory

I wrote it all—from the beginning
In postmodern score
Laced in hairspray and bass lines
That we stomped terrible love against the floor

~~I black out.~~

The Artist

An artful vagrant
A taxi line poetic
Constantly writing from his mental library
Where biker gangs gather for fist fights

A gas station arsonist
Holding a match
Well—
It's a sin to steal innocence
But such purity can be preserved in death
Isn't he romantic?
Pharmacy aisle panic sets in at midnight
When he gets jealous of the moon
Because it shines for you
Peeling away at peppered reflections
Along ghost crab tracks

One day it'll make sense

Until then
Ink will brand him
In hopes that geometry
Can speak louder than he

Time

We know as much about letting go
                As we do about growing old

I'm Just Being Honest

I'm sick of this silence
And how it cradles me to bed

I fall in love
Just to have the chance to regret

That might be the most honest thing
I've written yet

Too Late For Me

I want to write you clean
And sin free
Darling,
But these demons have me hanging on hooks
Dressed in costumed personalities
It's too late for me
I'm only alive
Because they like to read my poetry
Now
Let my lungs stre---------------tch to the cracks in your heart

Death Is A Mere Criticism Of Morality

I'm just the recycled bones
Of a Salvador painting
Dismantling winter
In a dead man's shoes
Along thoughts of human bondage
And our ties to forethought grifter's
Trading living for reality
Goddamn
Death is a mere criticism of morality

Aokigahara, Japan

Your passion captivated me
Like a canyon under a full moon
But I've always been Halloween

And
Sweet words do rot my teeth

Patience is just a second match
Said the Alchemist
Transmogrified into a realist

And
I am a hunter
Wearing a target at 3am
When introspection grabs my hand
Just to guide me into Aokigahara, Japan

First Crush

Sat calm in the field by my house
Watching you comb your hair with matches—
Legs drawing circles in that gasoline pond
                    I never got it

Until I discovered alcohol and pheromones
Letter jackets and sociological loop holes
I still dive and swim
Hoping to catch a glimpse,

                    Of love.

We never caught fire
Maybe we weren't trying hard enough?
A hard-shell community wagged by
Taking stock of meaning
Taunting the proverbial finish line
We live too much like lit cigarettes
But really—
Isn't that the safer bet?

Book Collector

Walls and walls of books.

They swelled at the middle of each rack; anyone could
tell they were forced too tightly between each end. Pages
between bindings, stacked tall as the trees cut down to print
them. They became unbalanced at the top of each chimney
spine and began to waterfall and rainbow to the floor. She had
no need for people, or so she said. If you were to ask her why
she had so many books, she'd merely smile and say,

"Some girls collect shoes."

You wouldn't press her to explain anymore because she had
one of those faces. Big brown eyes and high cheek bones
that swoop downward like a peach. I always found her face
fitting, with a chin like a comma. It draws you in intently, and
then you wait for anything that comes next. Biographies and
Greek Mythology courted poetry collections and binders full
of scholarly articles on psychopathy.

She told me once,

*"These books are orphans and I give them a place they won't
be ignored."*

      I learned more about her in that once statement than
most husbands know about their wives.

Believe In Your Spirit

There will be days some will be lost and others full of meaning. There will be days where you've conjured so many ghosts that you start to feel like one. Other days you'll make perfect sense of all that happens between breakfast, and falling asleep feeling productive. Some of these days you will win and others you will lose. DO NOT wear destiny like a noose. See, some of these days you'll remember the smell of coffee, and others you'll regret getting out of bed. But, I promise you this. I want to watch you watch the sunrise. I'm not just rooting for you. I'm beside you experiencing it. Together we will make it. Believe in your spirit.

Best And Worst Of Times

In the valleys of the young
We sprout wings
And play Irish folk songs
About kings
With lucky eyes
We take a drink
Raise one for those before
And one for those soon to be

We've got smoke inside our lungs
We've got bullets behind our tongues
We love like hate is hard to find
We simplify the greying line
Oh—
These are the best and worst of times

To Quarantine Hindsight

I'm staring at the furniture again
It doesn't move
Which reminds me a lot of my old friends

What a brushfire we were
Always trying to quantify our existence
The very attempts of which
Quarantined our potential

Now we're has been musicians
And full time poets playing pretend
Writing on our shins
In foreign languages
To prove we're not love impotent

Dirty Things

We're all dirty things
Searching
For a breath of something clean

I know someone
Who can feed me love,
But it doesn't taste like anything

She wore happiness
Like a stained wedding dress
And said,
"Deep down, we're all borrowed and blue
Not a soul loves anyone more than love itself,

Not even you.

Who Her

Watched you getting skinny for your suitors
Veins exposing on newly stretched skin

Rewind:
I was rich with love
You were emotionally vacant

Present Tense:
I'm a widower's chest
You're a fraternity mattress

Sold A Generation

Camera antenna
Radio lens
Leasing the housing market
On a drunken economy
Licking our wounds
Out of shot glasses
Rimmed with lime and sugar
Oh lustful normalcy
What are you really?
A sunken foundation with maintenance fees
Paid for by blisters and ankle casts—
A beggar with a broken wrist
Asking God for a better family?

The yard sale is really selling our dreams.
Keep your adoption down there
I'm breathing just fine out here

Identities and Ideologies

Oh, east coast enclave—
I drink to the hiraeth of it all
Like sending
  Junky dreamers to a blood bank
Like giving
  Drunk drivers' red lights
That's what happens
When a mother teaches a son
How to tithe his love

Palm trees pushed out of sanctioned dreams
We couldn't get very far
If evangelical ideologies
Gave birth to West coast identities

I mean—they started it all!

Rebel; like the supinely supreme
Sucking down wine glasses
On Harvard steps
Postulating death under columned monuments
About how it's all preserved

Maybe our swan songs
Were sung in the maternity ward

Dollhouse

Cotton balls shoved down my throat
A kindness
Oh, the imagination
Take the brain, but leave the heart
The rest—
Pour into a mold
Of chocolate window frames
And foreign holidays
                    I baptize myself in shame

Darling dollhouse
You only wear skin tight dresses
Because you never learned how to hold a pen
I've met you in the same bars
In different countries
                    Flirting with the same men
                              For some bar-stool conviction

Worry not love, I understand your story
To me you're still poetic
                    And beautifully written

Free Will

    I ~~was~~ the accident

God's decision for wisdom teeth (it was me)
Bones that atrophy (it was me)
Mysteries of the human heart
And more so
The soft space between
    Psychology and female sexuality (it was me)

Hieroglyphic attitude
Boasting a mystics aptitude
Societal faith resting on intangible fault lines
Love drawn in chalk—
    All un-chargeable crimes

    I ~~am~~ the accident

Human Bondage

Black widow on a pickled porch step
I see you, but you see—
Philosophy;
Existentialism;
Love in the murder capitol
With an automatic weapon swoon
Like kindness exists under a blood moon
Rage rats in a mirror maze
Hooked on the pleasure centers
Of their brains
Let's just call them humans
And they're really just—
Being
Is the punishment, judgement?

A scowling owl with eyes one would beg to fall in

Maybe daddy didn't do the things she says he did
She just fell in love with attention
      And then again
           Maybe he did
Either way,
Society will harness her to a synthetic wall

We All Carry A Mountain

I wrote a poem
To explain the necessity of
White blood cells
In an attempt to understand people
And their separate levels of Hell
How—
Giving a canvas to a camera man
Doesn't lower the cliff for the artist

But that's the thing about surviving
The perspective

Drunken lullabies in suburbia
Can be just as loud
As the ghetto wind

It's not the height of comparison
But the realization
That we all carry a mountain

Aging

I died today
In a foreign land
Drinking sand
From idle hands

I died today
In the metaphors
I wrote when I was young
After I was too old
To remove the rings
From inside the Oakwood

Says The Son

My iron lung rests next to the fireplace
Machines correcting your grammar
As daylight steals more time than it gives

The clock your father passed down
Swings through this shifting room
Like it knows the future
Better than you

And we better get to dying soon
Because midnight is the husk of dawn
Says the sun
Says the Son

The path to least resistance
Is through cardboard boxes
And filled chalices
Putting pain on ice
And stitching memories to lost time
The kind we never look for
Nor hope to find

...L i k e

Snow drift pep talks
Exposing neuropeptides

Like memory loss
      Like family estrangement
        Like blood loss

Espresso shots under fluorescent whites
Egg shells beneath headache conversations
Flashback Fridays and floral arrangements
We're all dying or getting married in a sauna

Love is a hot bath
Exposing trance trips at the rocky bottom

Like ocean tides
      Like college graduation
        Like pension payments

Burnt (Lying To Ourselves)

Clobbered your cultish fairytale
Bludgeoned it
Until it resembled drunk sex

Dried the wet dreams
Ironed your memories
Until they burned ugly dark spots
Into your psyche
      I made you wear them home

You were not even a souvenir
No—
You were coffin draped
Day old coffee soaked ribs
Wish-bone released
Always holding the smallest piece
You can't cry Amen
When you knew who you climbed into bed with

Now, say again
What didn't you expect?

Devotion

I'm a fool for the empty
   For fortunate goodbyes
   And empathetically bent replies
I'm a fixture in the room
Hardly noticed and heavily used
Fill me with love
Out of necessity; not desire
One stays with age
The other believes in constant change
I'm devoted to the incongruent stars
The falling ones
Who refuse to admit their death
I'm an antique bottle carrying a lover's wish
Across the ocean
And I will reach you
...Regardless

The Man On The Hill

The wind sang songs in this town
Of what?
Of dried oatmeal tossed on frat lawns
From spirits of future selves
That these tricky loyalists will never meet
Crushing oranges with the "Greek"
Along mahogany bars
With jalapeño peppered hearts
And saliva glands so spiritual
That Niagara Falls looks like a sprinkle
Clam baked junkies in their polo shirts
      Juggernaut fathers and neck tied victims
Too high to tell the difference between
      Value and valued
With valium stuffed ventricles
They devalue the art school Stepford's
Drinking sex on the beach
Through Benjamin Franklin straws
I'm a scarecrow on the hill
A plaid shirt stuffed with my own flaws
An observationalist with a liberal lust
For hating the way society sees nothing
Nothing but the man on the hill

We Were Younger

We were younger men
Clayed before apothecaries
Living off the winds of poverty
—Belligerently

We spoke of art before it spoke to us
Over syrup and cheap beer mornings
Car crashed and chipped statues
In tidy museums of little loves
Half forgotten
And posthumously beloved

I'm a few limed rims short
Of believing the spectacle
In the whispers etched in the spines I've broken
        Heroes became bones of those before
And I realized we're all models living in
Outdated generational trends

And I'll scatter
        In the wind
                Well I'd rather,
Like a timeless song from a nameless band
Before I burn out like some sorrowed family man

Poets

Keep me safe in your ashtray
Where your fingers
Won't linger
Too far away.

We're all killing ourselves darling
The Poets quicker than all
Because we've uncircumcised eyes
Constantly
Making
    Love
        To the
           Fall

About The Author

Patrick D. Hart is an unfiltered poet hailing from Newport News, Virginia. This collection of poetry is his bold attempt to connect with all truths, ugly and otherwise. He has an unhealthy obsession with writing, coffee and marshmallows.

Reach out and explore more of his work through Instagram or e-mail at pdhartpoetry@yahoo.com

CPSIA information can be obtained
at www.ICGtesting.com
Printed in the USA
BVOW03s0829050917
493997BV00001B/30/P